Station Stop

Station Stop

A Collection of Haiku and Related Forms

Richard Tice

Sumie *by A. Aiko Horiuchi*

Middlewood Press
Salt Lake City, Utah

Printed in the United States of America

First printing February 1986

ISBN 0-935961-00-3
Library of Congress Card Catalog Number 85-90484

To the Japanese people,

whom I love

Contents

Preface

This collection of haiku and related forms portrays an eight-year journey starting in Japan, circling through the western United States, and returning to Japan. When I first arrived in Ōsaka, I was a missionary who knew little Japanese and had to learn it while working among the people. Japan itself consists of four major islands, and I was assigned first to the smallest, Shikoku, which is reached from Honshu, the largest, primarily by ferry. After that I worked in the Kansai area, comprising Ōsaka, Kōbe, and Kyotō. With my return to the States, represented in this work by the Pacific Coast and the Great Basin, I began a serious study of Japanese literature and a few years later obtained a position teaching English at a small foreign language school in Maebashi (Jōshū area), northwest of Tōkyō (Kantō area).

I wrote most of the haiku in this collection during my last stay in Japan after I had finally learned to read and write some Japanese. Each haiku, poem, and personal essay is a stop along the way. The introduction, too, is part of the journey that moved me deeper into a Japanese experience I tried to reflect in English. Interestingly, the personal essay that begins the journey was one of the last pieces written. The impressions of that bewildering and ultimately reassuring boat-and-train ride to Matsuyama have remained with me vividly. It was in December, almost eight years to the date, as I was toying with the *haibun* form of personal essay, that I got the first two words. That day the rest followed, but it didn't flow out; I had to root it out line by line. The *haibun* that ends the collection was written three months before departure when I knew I would be leaving Japan, perhaps for a long time. It is another emotional piece, the result of leaving one land I had rapidly grown to love in favor of another, native-born love.

Acknowledgments

These poems and essays first appeared in the following publications:

Anthology of Western World Haiku Society—1979: "dark before the storm";

Anthology of Western World Haiku Society—1980: "moving out";

Bonsai: "evening trout-splash";

Cicada: "a crow caws," "a locust shell," "closing my eyes," "down worn stone," "funeral chant," "midnight in summer," "moving together," "nearer divorce," "rain," "red persimmons," "sailing off," "sunset caught," "the stark square campus buildings," "wish I were";

Climbing Ladders: "faint echo," "twin seagulls";

Dragonfly: "a hermit crab," "at the top," "by the kelp buckets," "eyeglasses: the world," "rain on oak leaves," "spider strands," "the rooster crows," "thunder roll," "wheels churning home," "winter rain";

Frogpond: "a blind friend," "back bent over," "bed-ridden wife," "black ahead," "Bridal Veil Falls," "desert smoke," "office-bound," "putting the hose away," "raising the stops," "spider web at dawn," "stars at dusk," "street snow," "the empty room," "What are those birds";

Inscape: "Search";

Japanophile: "Retreat of the Taira";

Mainichi Daily News: "a dog watches," "among autumn stars," "dry leaves rattle," "on a spread-out map," "Only the snow";

Modern Haiku: "afternoon rain," "Easter morning at Kannonyama," "etching," "late summer sunlight," "laughing," "night in the sickroom," "night rain," "November trout," "rising toward," "shivering," "summer rain," "Sunrise crinkling," "*Tatami,*" "the telephone wire";

Other Voices in American Poetry—1980: "Circling seagull," "New Year's Day";

Outch: "awaiting the train," "brushpoint poised," "first sleepless night," "hailstones strike," "heat-born breeze," "now the wild geese," "the halo";

Poetry Nippon: "drawn into sky," "Enkakuji," "morning walk," "in a black sky";

Tweed: "moonlit haze," "night snow";

Yomiuri Shimbun: "*Matsushima no.*"

Many thanks to Jack Lyon for his expert editing and to Karen Morales and Kent Ware for their excellent advice on design and production.

inazuma ya
yami no kata yuku
goi no koe
Bashō

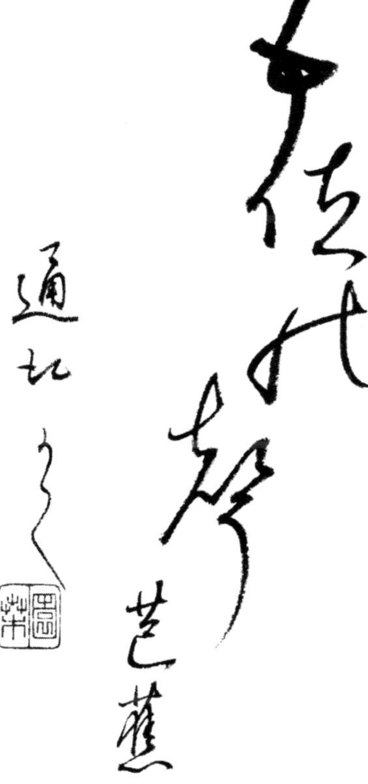

Calligraphy by Iizuka Michie
Translation on page 11

Introduction
Haiku: From Japanese into English

I thought I wrote my first "haiku" in 1970. Early one odd morning, a dream I was having suddenly formed into three related poems—I could see them on the paper—and I awoke, recording the words while they were still in mind. Each poem consisted of 5-7-5-7-7 syllable lines about nature—I called them tanka because that was what I had been taught in high school. A few months later I showed them to one of my English professors at Berkeley. He liked the poems but called them haiku, commenting that the form was difficult.

Of course, the poems were neither tanka nor haiku; though likeable as short poems, they conformed to only one of the rules that constitute either form. Ironically, that rule on syllable count (5-7-5 for haiku, 5-7-5-7-7 for tanka) is the only rule not applicable in English. Traditionally, Japanese haiku do require five syllables for the first line, seven for the second, and five for the third; and even modern haiku, while sometimes deviating from this count, operate on a recognized standard. The Japanese language itself, however, counts syllables differently from English: a syllable consists of a consonant plus vowel, with the exception of isolated vowels and the ending consonant *n*. For instance, the word *daikon,* a large white radish, would be two syllables in English—*dai-kon*—but four in Japanese—*da-i-ko-n*.

More importantly, Japanese haiku are six to eight words average, whereas English "haiku" of 5-7-5 syllables average twelve to fourteen words, primarily because English is comprised of mono- and polysyllabic words while Japanese is largely polysyllabic. Moreover, Japanese haiku do not use punctuation but instead rely on special words (*kireji*) included in the syllable count that end, emphasize, or convey pauses. (I don't know of any poets writing in English who count punctuation as syllables.) Essentially then, these linguistic differences make the 5-7-5 syllable line poem too wordy in English.

Luckily, my interests and work took me to Japan twice; and since that embarrassing start in 1970, I have tried to learn much more about the form, using new principles of haiku in my writing as I encountered them. To date I have written approximately one hundred and seventy-five haiku and twenty-five *senryū,* of which about eighty have appeared in small periodicals in the United States, Canada, Japan, and Australia. Most of these, plus two short *renga,* a narrative *renga* patterned on the poetry in Nō plays, and two *haibun,* appear in this collection. The haiku on page 17 is the only Japanese haiku of mine to be printed, but it has pleased me the most because it appeared in the haiku column of a large Japanese newspaper.

The previous terms *senryū, renga,* and *haibun* may be unfamiliar to some readers. By way of quick definition, a *senryū* is a variant of haiku, featuring human affairs and oftentimes wittiness. A *renga* is a form of linked verse, alternating stanzas of 5-7-5 and 7-7, each pair of stanzas forming an independent poem within the longer poem. Each stanza is connected to the previous stanza through mood, contrast, image, or verbal play. A *haibun* is a philosophic travelogue punctuated at moments of tension or perception by haiku.

Form

Some years ago, while trying to synthesize the principles of haiku coherently, I developed a rather involved working definition that has proven useful: a Japanese haiku is an objective, concrete poem usually of 5-7-5 syllable lines, consisting of two or three simple, juxtaposed images held in tension, acutely aware of moment and nature and being. I have also divided the rules and tendencies into five categories: structure, image, time, suggestiveness, and language. Not all the principles involved in Japanese haiku can be incorporated into English, but a great many can, while others could allow alteration or substitution.

Structure

Structure involves such things as syllable and word count, lineation and length of lines, resulting rhythm or flow, juxtaposition of images, and tension. The Japanese have a term for excessive syllables (*jiamari*) in lines, and six- or eight-syllable lines are occasionally used. The basic 5-7-5 form, though, gives meaning to lines that go beyond regulation, and Japanese poets must have good reason to break the rule. For instance, the second line of Bashō's first famous poem has nine syllables, which suggests the heaviness of the crow settling on the branch:

kareeda ni
karasu no tomaritaru ya
aki no kure

on a withered branch
the settling of a crow—
*autumn dusk**

The second example (a haiku written in the late 1970s) has a six-syllable third line:

taikan ni
horishi seireki
sakura no sono
Shugyō

in a thick trunk
is carved the Christian era:
the cherry orchard

---

*All translations are my own.

The third line is the only attractive, smoothly read line in a poem that portrays Western and Chinese influences on Japan. The mention of the Christian calendar and Chekhov's play *The Cherry Orchard* indicates, for example, Western cultural and literary influences. The effect that the Chinese writing system and Chinese pronunciation and vocabulary has had on Japanese is reflected in the use of Chinese ideograms for purely Japanese words, like *sakura* and *horishi,* and in the choice of Chinese readings where Japanese ones could have been used, as *taikan* instead of the Japanese reading *futomiki*. The poem demonstrates how much Japanese language, literature, and culture have been affected. The beauty of the last line, however, implies that the hybrid result is also aesthetically pleasing in its own way.

The 5-7-5 lineation in Japanese also creates a rhythm. Japanese is an unaccented language and entails only a slight raising or lowering of voice for pitch, so accented poetry and tonal poetry, like that in classical Chinese, are impossibilities. The syllabification, however, definitely establishes a flow, a wavelike motion caused by the short-long-short lines:

ware to kite *asobe ya oya no* *nai suzume* *Issa*	*Come to me* *and play, parentless* *young sparrow.*

Although haiku is printed in one vertical line in texts, the syllabification and resulting flow are always obvious, and calligraphic renditions usually break the poem into its three basic lines. However, the printed form of haiku has given rise to one-line poems in English; some haiku poets maintain that since the Japanese haiku is printed as one line with the breaks implicit in that line, English haiku should be similarly written. One-line English haiku are included regularly in many major North American haiku periodicals, such as *Modern Haiku* and *Frogpond*. Some, such as *Dragonfly,* seldom use it. I use the one-line haiku often, but only when the image or movement is linear, as in this one:

sailing off after the pale moon   white seagull

The problem of what structure to use in English has created the most interesting debate about the form. Although some poets still use 5-7-5 syllable lines, the majority follow Blyth's suggestion in *Haiku* of using short-long-short lines with a maximum syllable count of seventeen. I frequently use a variation of Blyth's form: I try for short-long-short lines with a maximum word count of nine and no single line over five or seven syllables. For a while I experimented with 3-5-3 syllable haiku, like this:

Faint echo—
a mallard? wild geese?
thunder breaks.

I feel the terseness and basic resemblance to the Japanese form help duplicate its tempo and timing (flow). Still, English haiku poets have tried many variations, the three most common being short-short-long, long-long-short, and long-short-long. Whatever the form, most poets maintain a limit of seventeen syllables. Though I have tried various syllable-length lines, I have yet to find a combination that has the natural ease 5-7-5 has in Japanese.

Along with the three lines, the substance or content of the haiku itself has two parts, the juncture ordinarily coming at the end of the first line,

tabi ni yande // yume wa kareno o / kakemeguru
Bashō

fallen ill on the road   dreams weave through desolate fields in the middle of the second (see page 4 for translation),

ware to kite / asobe ya // oya no / nai suzume

or at the end of the second (see page 3 for translation),

kareeda ni / karasu no tomaritaru ya // aki no kure.

Most often these parts are images rather than commentary or stated feelings; furthermore, the images are typically disparate, related only by the immediate experience and almost never causally (by cause and effect). This juxtaposition of two disparate fragments of an experience, if done well, will both evoke the entire experience with its emotion and create tension. Tension in haiku is difficult to describe: in some way the two elements resonate or vibrate within the poem and against each other. The tension stems both from juxtaposition and the qualities of the images and causes a static poem to become dynamic.

Image

Images provide the essential content in haiku and usually number two or three per poem. Quite naturally because of length limitations, no image is extended or even developed. Images do, however, suggest an overall setting. Here reader participation is necessary to complete the missing parts. The following contemporary haiku has three images—the bird, the ripples, and the spring—but marsh grasses or reeds, some boulders, leafless trees, stillness and silence, absence of animal life are all evoked by the primary images:

tori mo mare no fuyu no izumi no aomizuwa
Rinka

and a rare bird in a blue ripple of a winter spring

The setting develops from what words like "rare" and

"winter" evoke, from what would naturally and logically be in the setting, and from what the reader imagines.

Quite often the last is the most important. Donald Keene in *World within Walls* tells the story of Bashō's most famous haiku. After Bashō had composed the second and third lines first—"*kawazu tobikomu / mizu no oto*" (a frog jumps in / water-sound)—Kikaku suggested "*yamabuki ya*" (yellow roses) for the first line. That, however, was finally abandoned in favor of "*furuike ya*" (ancient pond). Yet Aiko Horiuchi, the *sumie* artist for this collection, told me she once did a well-received illustration of the poem using a willow tree.

Furthermore, poets seldom include subjective interpretation. This objectivity, as in the preceding haiku by Rinka, prevents the poet from imposing his interpretation upon the images and allows the reader to perceive them personally. The poet, then, is nonegocentric: every facet of nature, including man, is equally important and vital. This does not mean poets cannot be part of their haiku, but it does lead them to establish focal points outside themselves. In Issa's poem (page 4), the situation moves from pitiful Issa and pitiful sparrow to a middle point of mutual encouragement:

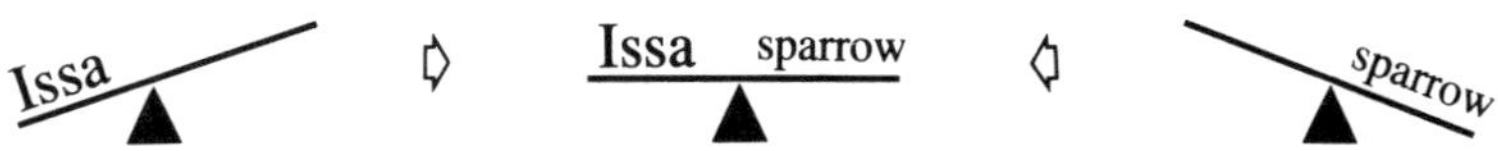

Bashō's poem on dreams (page 5) has the images interrelated in a fashion that resembles a crosscut circle:

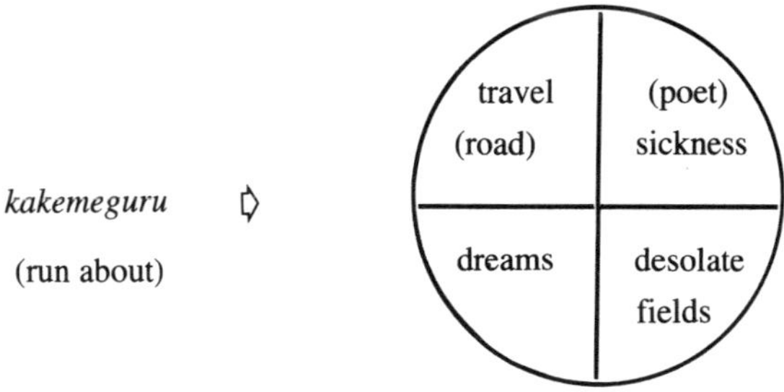

Images in haiku are also concrete, with words used self-sufficiently (i.e., the word *oak* need not be modified; it should recall the object sufficiently). Figurative images such as metaphor, simile, and personification are few, though occasionally found in modern haiku. In one sense, figurative images are restrictive, no matter how spectacular they might be. To call the moon an opal among stars may be imaginative, and the reader might not think of it otherwise; nevertheless, the moon becomes that object and that only—its impact on the reader is narrowed.

If used, figurative images are based upon concrete images, with a natural feel maintained in the poem, and the departure is justified by a suitable reason:

bara ikusen *fureyo yuki furu* *yoru no umi* Yukei	*Thousands of roses,* *fall! Snow falling on* *night sea*

The metaphor of roses for snow is juxtaposed against the night sea and the snow itself. Even with this metaphor the poem follows the common technique of linking through experience naturally dissociated or conflicting elements, such as winter/summer, the permanent and eternal with the mutable and temporary, color/noncolor, in a balance that creates tension. One common theme of haiku is unity in disparity, and thus the metaphor also presents the wholeness of experience: the subjective and objective as one. Though this haiku is atypical in imagery, its movement is not. Haiku poets typically approach the internal through the external, and the subjective through the objective.

Time

Probably the second most famous rule after the 5-7-5 syllable structure is the season word (*kigo*). This rule is actually part of a larger consciousness of time and its effect upon life and the world.

na no hana ya
tsuki wa higashi ni
hi was nishi ni
Buson

菜の花や月は東に日は西に

mustard blossoms . . .
moon in the east
sun in the west

The time is the present, in the evening in spring. As Buson's eyes wander over the wide expanse of yellow blossoms on a green background, he notices first the moon rising in the east and then the sun setting in the west. This sets the time at dusk, with the colors darkened by the evening. The entire experience is anchored in spring by the common sight of the flowering mustard (*na no hana,* the season word, is actually a plant that resembles the edible mustard).

The delicate balance in time of flowers, rising moon, and setting sun—three transitory objects that are nevertheless permanent in their regular reappearances—creates an overwhelming feeling of mutability and the eternal. This feeling of constant reappearance is emphasized by Buson's clever alternation of Chinese characters and Japanese sound syllables (*hiragana*), creating a pattern like this: o·o·o·o·o·o·. The moment in the haiku will vanish quickly but will reappear someplace each evening, each spring, again and again.

This immediacy of experience is largely conveyed by the use and awareness of time. Verbs in haiku will almost always be in a present tense, and one or more words will suggest the season. Season words may be obvious (such as *winter* or *spring*), indicative of the season in which they belong (such as *cherry blossoms* or *snow*), or suggestive of the season by conventional usage (such as *ants* for summer, *moon* for autumn). In addition, haiku might mention day or night, morning or evening, though these are often omitted. The images themselves, however, reflect some quality of time: eternal, transitory, or both (like waves); changing, nonchanging, or everchanging. For instance, cherry blossoms are ephemeral and ethereal, but Shugyō's use of the trunk in the haiku on page 3 suggests the durability of the cherry (the traditional symbol of Japan) in weathering change.

The quality of time works as well in English as in Japanese, but season words must be native to their regions. Dried grasses in Japan, for example, often indicate winter, whereas in California they indicate summer. Frogs in the western United States also recall summer, but in Japan they can signify spring because of their sudden noisy awakening from hibernation when the rice fields are first flooded. No matter what images are used, they are always anchored consciously or unconsciously in the poet's perception of time and its place in life.

Suggestiveness

Japanese poets use numerous techniques to make their haiku more suggestive. One technique that frequently disappears in translation is the pivot word (*kakekotoba*), a word that expands, multiplies, or deepens meaning. Sometimes I can't decide which Japanese word is pivotal because I don't know the connotations and alternate meanings, and even when I think I know which word is, the openness is often nontransferable to English. This poem by Issa is an example:

tomokaku mo	*At any rate,*
anata makase no	*this year of giving in to you*
toshi no kure	*has ended*

At first this seems like a humorous twist on New Year's Eve poems and a sarcastic observation about Issa and his wife's relationship. However, the tone of resignation in *tomokaku* (anyway) and the association of *kure* (ending) with *anata* (you) suggest his wife's death. Subsequent readings reinforce the inference that his wife has died this year. On New Year's Eve, when the rituals and habits of family life are especially pronounced, Issa is apparently trying to cheer himself as he sits before the family altar containing a picture of his wife, facing the prospect of a lonely year.

Other times the pivot word is more obvious because of double meanings, as this modern haiku by Kokyō:

inazuma ya	*Lightning flash!*
fukete hanayagu	*night deepens, a woman's*
onna no koe	*voice grows cheerful . . .*

Hanayagu, besides meaning cheerful or lively, also means coquettish, which considerably alters the mood and experience. But in addition to this, the poet also uses allusion to open the poem further. He is playing on a famous haiku of Bashō by using some of the words, similar sounds, and a parallel grammatical stucture:

inazuma ya	*Lightning flash!*
yami no kata yuku	*going into the darkness,*
goi no koe	*a night heron's cry . . .*

He establishes a direct contrast between the disembodied voices: one is mysterious, almost supernatural; the other, corporeal, tied strongly to the body and life.

Kokyō's use of pivot words, allusion, and association is common to other poets and is duplicable in English. In my first published haiku, before I knew about pivot words, I used one accidentally:

evening trout-splash—
too late, only the wrinkling
water and echo

Here the word *late* means not only the lateness of day, but also the lateness of action—hearing the splash but always turning my head too late to see the trout. The allusion to Bashō's famous poem was also accidental:

furuike ya	*ancient pond—*
kawazu tobikomu	*a frog jumps in*
mizu no oto	*water-sound*

Syntactic ambiguity is common, too, in Japanese haiku. For example, relative clauses in Japanese are placed just before the nouns they modify. Bashō uses this grammatical construction for his haiku on the frog: "*kawazu tobikomu / mizu no oto*." The first two words could be read either as an independent sentence with a separate phrase for the following line or as a relative clause for the next three words. The first would be "a frog jumps in—water sound"; the second, "the water sound that the frog jumps into." He describes, then, simultaneously the way he perceives the action and the way it actually occurs. Bashō hears the sound first, then thinks of the frog, as if the sound preceded the action, reversing cause and effect.

Controlled ambiguity is even more frequent in Japanese poetry and is also a common element in English poetry. Since Japanese often eliminates the personal pronoun when it is understood, a poet can use this advantageously. In Bashō's poem on dreams (page 5), the "I" and "my" are omitted. The resulting slight dissociation of dreams from the dreamer creates a feeling of unearthliness. In Shugyō's poem on the cherry orchard (page 3), the reader naturally assumes the date has been carved in the trunk for some time, but the person looking at the date, possibly the poet, might have carved it him or herself.

From Bashō on, another device Japanese poets have used is "flavoring," sometimes called *nioi* (aroma, smell). *Nioi* creates an identifiable mood or flavor. Toward the end of his life, Bashō maintained that *karumi* (light taste) was the most desirable quality for haiku. This is the treatment of a serious subject with lightness or even humor. Issa's poem on his wife's death (page 10) is an example of this. *Yūgen* is another—a term for unearthliness, the mysterious; Bashō's poem of the night heron's cry (page 11) has this feel. Flavor words are peculiarly Japanese and difficult to translate or describe. Some others (with inadequate descriptions) are *mono no aware,* aesthetic sensibility for the pathos in things; *makoto,* sincerity or truth; *wabi,* taste for the quiet and simple; *sabi* (from *sabishisa,* loneliness), elegant simplicity suggestive of change and aloneness; and *shibumi,* astringency, severe exquisiteness. In English, *nioi* would be similar to a unified mood for each haiku. I sometimes use these Japanese "flavorings" to enrich the emotion and find that they do not necessarily make the haiku seem Japanese.

Language

As mentioned in the paragraphs on ambiguity, language is deliberately used to create richer poems. This in itself is distinctive to neither Japanese nor haiku, yet some particular uses of language in Japanese haiku are. One practice that is peculiar and easily imitated in English is the ratio of parts of speech to each other. Haiku is essentially a poem of nouns, often with one verb or at most two for action. In the eleven Japanese haiku discussed previously, there are forty-two nouns as compared to thirteen verbs, seventeen prepositions (most of which are *no* or *na,* used to indicate possession), twelve particles (parts of speech that indicate subject, object, emphasis, and so on), two conjunctions, two adverbs, one pronoun, and *no* adjectives. To be fair, however, Japanese poets largely avoid adjectives by using noun/noun combinations (like *kare/no*), which usually translate into English as adjective/noun (desolate fields). In the eleven haiku, there are eight such compound nouns. Furthermore, nouns in most haiku are concrete or nonconceptual (unlike *love* or *patriotism*), perceived through the senses or other definite means like time (*year*), measurement (*end*), or thought (*dream*).

Sound—assonance and alliteration—is also highly developed. Japanese has only five vowels, twenty simple consonants, and eleven compound consonants (like *ky* in *kya*). Lines like "*sakura no sono,*" "*yuki furu / yoru no umi,*" and intricate sound structure as in the following are typical:

tabi ni yande yume wa kareno o kakemeguru
1 2 2 31 4 3 4 1 51 4 6 6 5154 457 7

English has greater possibilities for sounds than Japanese, but inversely the number of different sounds can dilute the poem. Surprisingly, rhyme is almost nonexistent in Japanese poetry; and evidently it often creates an unfortunate artificial effect in English haiku. Tempo and the use of sound to reinforce mood or meaning are, however, usual among good Japanese haiku poets, particularly Buson. The following haiku, when read aloud, uses sounds to imitate the breeze that separates a petal from the flower ("*chitte*"), the petal's pause and slow falling ("*uchikasanarinu*"), and the separate, distinct piling up of two, then three petals ("*nisanpen*"):

botan chitte
uchikasanarinu
nisanpen
Buson

a peony scattering,
all piled up—
two, three petals

牡	*bo*
丹	*tan*
散	*chi*
つ	*(tsu)*
て	*te*
う	*u*
ち	*chi*
か	*ka*
さ	*sa*
な	*na*
り	*ri*
ぬ	*nu*
二	*ni*
三	*san*
片	*pen*

Japanese also has a fascinating visual effect in its language that English unfortunately cannot duplicate in a natural way. The combination of Chinese ideographs (*kanji*) and the Japanese syllabary (*hiragana,* a set of simplified characters for the forty-six basic syllables in Japanese) can emphasize words, suggest images and meanings, or imitate actions. In Buson's haiku, traditionally written from top to bottom, the eye first meets the peony (*botan*); encounters the ideograph for falling (*chi*), which consists of two parts—one representing the bamboo, the other, separation; then follows a string of *hiragana* pictorially duplicating the downward, dancelike fall of light petals that settle into the ideograph for two (二, *ni*), then three (三, *san*). I wish this visual richness were available in English, but it is not, and as a result I have only occasionally been able to suggest faint representations of the image, such as this haiku:

dark before the storm—
dandelion puffs
floating free

Some poets are working more with "eye-ku"—poems using letters and other typewriter marks to create shapes on the page—but I feel that the variant is too artificial to suit the naturalness of haiku.

Explication

Most of Japan's literary genres require informed readers, yet haiku has the advantage of immediate accessibility on a primary level. Without much training or effort, readers can appreciate the images and the subtle effects of tension and structure. It isn't difficult, however, to read the genre for depth. One poet I know in Tokyo once characterized haiku as a world in a drop of water. I think that is absurd: haiku is not simple-minded, but neither is it so deep as to boggle the senses.

For those who don't know what to do with a haiku when they reach the end much sooner than they had anticipated, I have included a list of questions to answer. These are the steps I use when I find a haiku that intrigues me, though reading for depth, of course, is not nearly so formal as the steps may suggest:

1. What is the overall setting?
2. How do the lineation, rhythm, and sound work?
3. Are there any pivot words, deliberate ambiguity, and allusions?
4. What are the qualities of the images, and how do the images work with each other?
5. How does the haiku present time?
6. What are the mood and emotion?

I would also add that I read the poem aloud several times during the analysis.

These questions are fairly easy to apply. As an example, I'd like to examine the following haiku of mine (calligraphy on facing page), which most non-Japanese readers would not understand without an explication anyway:

Matsushima no
kuroumi ni uku
yakōuki

in Matsushima's black sea floats a luminescent float

Matsushima means "pine islands," but in the blackness of night and sea, the islands cannot be seen. The only thing that can is a tiny red light rising and ebbing with the heaving of the waves. Somewhere watching the float is a fisherman, also unseen. The lineation is standard (5-7-5), and the rhythm matches the wave motion. The vowel sounds in "*yakōuki*" also create a feeling of rising and falling as they are formed in the throat and mouth. The most obvious combinations of sounds are *ku—uku* and *umi—uku—uki*. The noun "*uki*" (float, bobber) is formed from the verb "*uku*" (to float), but the word recalls through its Chinese ideograph the *ukiyo* (floating world) predominant in the Edo period: a

松島の
黒海にうく
夜光浮

world of fleeting pleasures and dreams centered in Edo (now Tokyo) and Ōsaka.

Matsushima itself is one of the two or three most known, admired spots in Japan, dotted offshore by numerous, craggy pine islands. The area was also the highlight of Bashō's most famous literary journey, which he commemorated with this poem:

Matsushima ya	*Matsushima!*
Aa Matsushima ya	*Ah Matsushima,*
Matsushima ya	*Matsushima!*

Bashō's deceptively simple haiku plays on the irony of the situation: he has traveled the length of Japan to see the islands, composing along the way what he has felt to be some of his best work; yet when he finally arrives, the sight, relief, and joy render him incapable of anything more than a straightforward exclamation. His poem also sets up an arresting rhythm in an otherwise rhythmless language. Bashō's haiku on Matsushima plays on the name, occurs during the day, and depends on sight; in direct contrast, my haiku of Matsushima occurs in the dark and obliterates sight. The two associated together imply that experience cannot be restricted, can be anywhere and anytime.

The sea is powerful—overpowering—black, huge, expansive, but the float is nevertheless all the more observable by its singleness and contrasts: light/dark, weak/powerful, small/huge, transient/permanent, manmade/natural. Yet despite its insignificance, it exists as palpably as the sea. The contrast is strengthened by the ideographs for *yakō* (luminescence): *ya* means evening, *kō* means light. To a lesser extent, the pairings of ideographs for pine islands and for black sea also emphasize the contrast. The images, however polarized or unrelated they seem, are naturally linked by the ordinary livelihood of fishing: an ordinary linking for extraordinary qualities.

The time is summer—the sea turns black in parts of

Northern Japan in summer—night, the present, and the limits of time seem to stretch without end. The float is transitory, the sea is eternal, yet both move together, the float subservient to the sea, though the motion of the sea can be observed only through the motion of the float. The mood is a combination of loneliness, unearthliness, and affirmation in negation. As a final step I would usually leave the poem for a few days in order to forget the analysis, then return to it for a fresh look. Haiku seems to work best when experienced rather than analyzed, as I hope the following *haibun* and haiku will work for the reader.

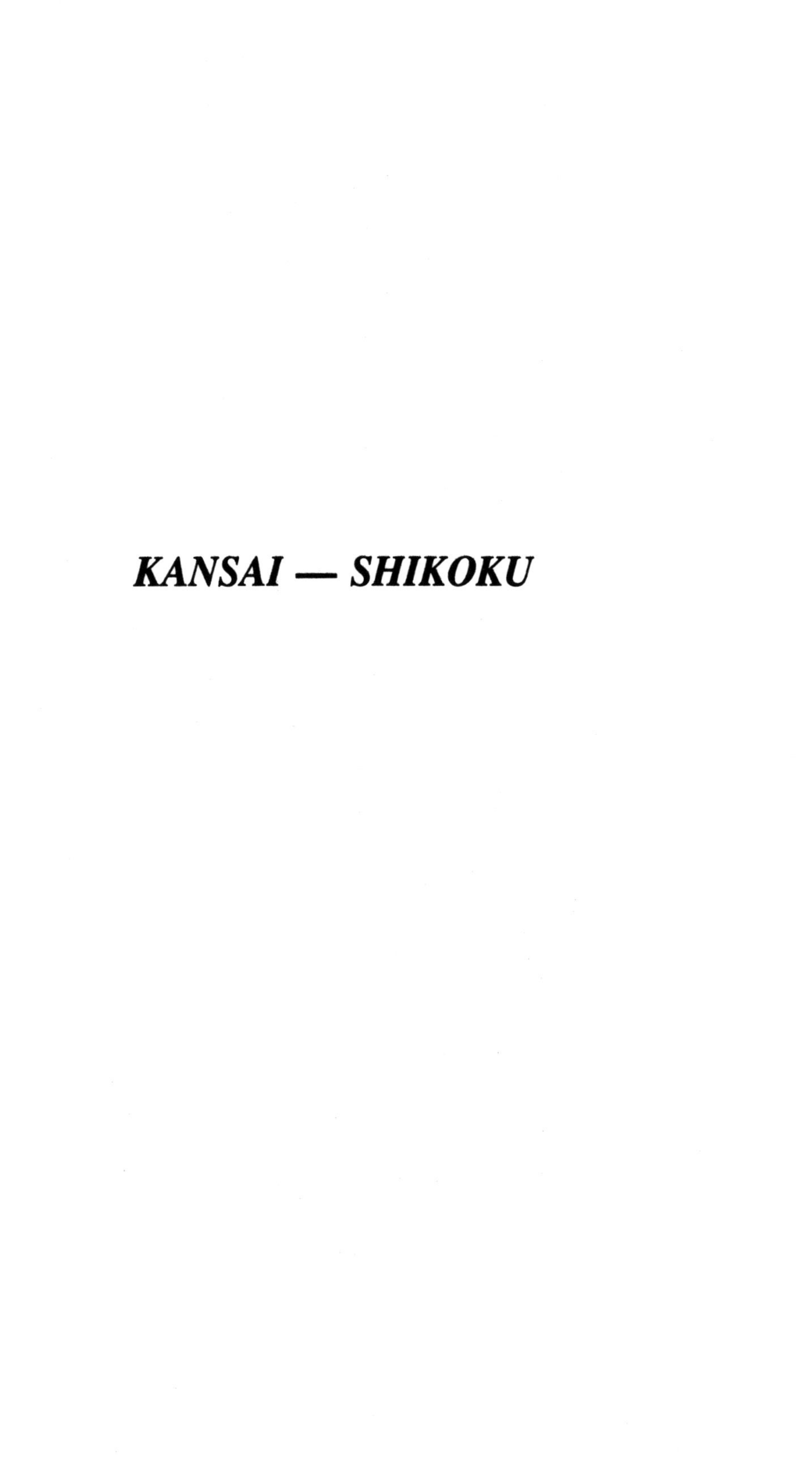

KANSAI — SHIKOKU

Search

December. Ōsaka. Every word a world. Damp, cold, each building wrapped in it. Evening. Far off where the outlines of the city have disappeared, red yellow white lights burn unsteadily like vacillating fires on a well of black ice. A fine mist of rain sinks on the grey buildings, and the unmoving silver plane has become grey, too, as we move away. Some speak, but all words fade as we walk further into the land. Ōsaka. December.

Mina wa tsukarete iru deshō. No. Yes. Irresolute, weary. Rest for tomorrow, then after? *Kochira no hō e kite itadakimasu ka?* We strain through the sounds: people swarm through the huge lobby, directionless. Light is dissipated through the windows—the windowpanes are hard: two branches knock against one. Inside, aimless echoes of souls sift and turn around us; we wait, we move into the harsh winter again.

Two days after. Steel-grey water ahead. The boat rolls, now and again slaps the waves, sometimes rocks fitfully. Though land behind and before has ceased in the drizzling haze, to the right is Awaji. The island is black: the forest slides by, billowing in the dark; the town caught on the edge of sea is charcoal—room lights flutter like moths around dusk. Even light from the passenger room seems uncertain, and on the walkway people come to huddle, smell the sodden air, and leave.

rain; colder on the ferry far from home   long trailing wake

We watch the wisps of white on the caps of waves.

Two are left now. Our hands push against the window; one platform down, some others enter another train. Takamatsu—Kochi, Takamatsu—Tokushima, and others have stayed here. The engine shudders, our coach shudders, then the train eases out toward Matsuyama. There is some blue in the sky. An ivy climbs the left wall—a few tendrils disappear into shadow. Water-streaked buildings fuse, faces blur within and without, movement stretches the country into one color; only the sea stands clear. Some men are casting nets through which the water runs.

Ever in motion: cold men and women at night, bundled in grey coats, lustreless. The streets are confused, always people walking one way or another; between the streetlamps, shadows. Only one dog under one light searches the faces of passersby. Occasionally a car sends a sheet of water from the street to the sidewalk. Trees with tightly clipped branches line the fronts of buildings. Not far from the station: above, a white, aluminum sign with words we know but cannot yet read; below, unpainted wood. The entrance is open.

He and I are on the seashore. Two roofless dressing stalls are covered with umbrellas. Laughter beyond; there is excitement here, too. Towels lie on the wet sand, cold seeps from the concrete walls, against the chill and empty sound of drops we dress in white. The ocean murmurs. Outside again. Others, smiling, have newly come from the train station; all move toward the undulating sea washing heavily onto the sand. Behind, the train rumbles, a line of lights moves out and fades. All pause where the water falls back; two continue, stop, steady themselves against the rise and ebb of water, and face the shore.

New Year's Day;
in the rain between the waves
I baptize him

and we have found the fire in the cold.

the halo
and huge moon enfold
the knotted pine.

night rain
against the water, young rice
into the rain

late summer sunlight—
whispers in the chapel enjoin
the coffin's silence.

etching
the sun on water—
dragonfly shadow

hailstones strike
the iron streetlamp . . .
the light

awaiting the train
he looks at people
waiting for trains

on a spread-out map
a fly leaves the loop line
at Umeda

spider web at dawn
brilliant against ditch water
red begonias

down worn stone of temple steps   spring rain

moving together—
    noise of the bike, silence
        of the dragonfly

Retreat of the Taira

Toward Suma's shores,
the wild shores, we come driven,
winter winds blowing

through the seabirds' cries, to wake
by the desolate water.

Over scattered reeds
the wild geese fly yet southward,
following their course;

scattered men have come south too
till stopped by the restless waves.

Weary travelers
who hear the geese flying low
think of journey's end;

yet the traveler's hope fails
when the blowing wind chills him.

moving out—
in the bedroom, the hollow
sound of rain

first sleepless night—
frogs have taken over
flooded ricefields

shivering
from influenza:
long way home

a dog watches
every passing car:
autumn dusk.

night in the sickroom
the throbbing of my temple
and the crickets cry

THE PACIFIC COAST

dusk in the gully.
almost entering
the sound of crickets

hand over hand—
water sheeting
from the swaying crab net

rain on oak leaves—
sharing a cranny
with the ants

drawn into sky   the stars : the stars   drawn into sea

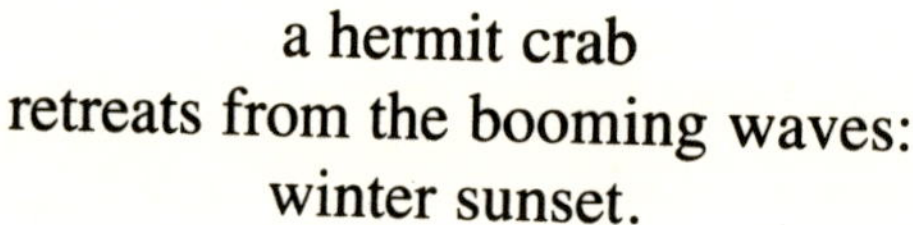

a hermit crab
retreats from the booming waves:
winter sunset.

twin seagulls
sailing off beyond dark water

sailing off after the pale moon white seagull

a blind friend tracing the crack on a vase—her hand
moves into sunlight

winter rain:
back in the bed I slept in
as a child

Sunrise crinkling
the foiled water: blaze of light
fills the taut line.

in a black sky,
under black water,
through black leaves: stars

eyeglasses: the world
so close every new leaf moves
against the others

faint echo—
a mallard? wild geese?
thunder breaks.

summer rain   wet shellfish thrown in the beach fire

Circling seagull;
neither wind nor wave has touched
the sand castle

by the kelp buckets
an old diver pulls an octopus
inside out

at the top—
dried thornbushes : from sand dunes
to the sea below

stars at dusk:
churning in the waves,
sea-bound smolt

house-lined hill
each step adds a breath
to night fog

a locust shell
clings to the dry weed;
a child cries

THE GREAT BASIN

raising the stops: kids race irrigation water down the dry trenches

Bridal Veil Falls:
all along the granite cliff—
summer sun

Only the snow,
and lights wink out one by
one this Eve.

Lightning!
stretch of sand between
dark and dark

the stark square campus buildings at the start of the winter moon

a crow caws:
morning sun sets on fire
all the icicles

desert smoke drifts from star to star   silence of water

the telephone wire sags from gathering swallows
road through the desert

What are those birds, white, suspended between sun and peak?

Dry leaves rattle
about the skeletal
scarecrow. thunder.

sheet lightning—
storm clouds feather
the half moon

office-bound:
through the apricot blossoms
late snow falling

heat-born breeze
scarcely stirs the aspen leaves;
motionless fish

the rooster crows:
through the dark, pale icicles
on the house eaves

putting the hose away: pumpkins
scattered through ruined tomato vines

low-flying crows;
lake water cools
the red cliffs burned into eyes

street snow   he looks at price tags on roses

back bent over the chimney stove, the old man listens to wind

thunder roll;
through the dry canyon
cloud shadows

just the silver sides
of an unfinished house
in miles of snow

from discarded evergreens
neighborhood children
still picking tinsel

night of no sound:
now and again the storm clouds
fill with light

weed-lined sidewalk:
glass shards anchor
this web of light . . .

even as rain
rattles the windows—
our neighbor's sprinkler

the wind-driven snow—
house after house after house
fades away to dreams

spider strands
    follow the sunflower's arc
        to the far sunrise

the empty room,
carnations on a table
by the opened card

November trout poled over fading charcoal   the mountain narrows

morning walk
through the neighborhood echoes
off fog-wrapped mountains

quaking aspen:
sun on lake water lost
to one more leaf

rising toward
the slow turn of maple seeds
the child's laughter

evening trout-splash—
too late, only the wrinkling
water and echo

JŌSHŪ — KANTŌ

now the wild geese
now the far-off child
call and call

black ahead.
my rearview mirror
fills with sun

through black smoke
from burning rice fields
two cranes—skyward

wish I were the ant in the crack of the cool stone wall too

midnight in summer
against a cinder-block wall
dandelion eyes

afternoon rain . . .
morning glories leave no trace
of fences

Enkakuji:

temple halls still;
around the massive bronze bell
hidden birdsong

the boom of struck metal—
sweating monks begin prayers

sunlight on leaves;
perched on the bellringing pole
red dragonfly

within the winter rain
echoes fading away . . .

brushpoint poised:
the students' hush anticipates
the old hand

closing my eyes
to the winter sun—
warm, red light

between these boulders
at Oni-oshi-dashi
worlds of red ants

sunset caught
    in the dried sunflower's arc
and torn web

funeral chant
for a distant someone;
pulsing blood . . .

bed-ridden wife
into her fourth day . . .
will the rain ever stop?

nearer divorce:
memories, words—
winter wind.

among autumn stars.
one star moves
as a child is born

Easter morning on Kannonyama:

flowering cherries—
we read from John
"When it was yet dark"

two petals then a third
come to rest on the page

red persimmons:
carrying in my arms
my sick child

laughing,
Kamakura's bronze buddha
fills with children

dark before the storm—
dandelion puffs
floating free

moonlit haze
silvers the whole sky—
road unfolding

spring tournament:
the black stone sounds
the pattern of *go*

wheels churning home,
the train lurches left—
snow-topped mountains!

night snow
sweeps the neighbor's yard—
home after years

Tatami

When the hours become habits and days spiral in familiar patterns, do we say then, "We are no longer strangers"? Each turn of the clock carries the land deeper into our hearts, and each word marks the moment we live. The silences also are full of words we will never utter. Our moments, too, are full of things fusing with our lives: pillows to cradle our heads each night, the halls that funnel our movements, walls which shape our waking hours. The path alongside my house has followed the same road for years but moves each day with me to my destination. Road, I will hate to leave you. Each day I see your cracks, the asphalt wet or dry; and the arguments fresh that morning, or the expectations arising new with the day, move silent down the stretch. You hold them for my return; and the stillness, the well-defined fences, fields, and sidewalks calm me.

I am no stranger to this land. The concrete and the green that I travel every day I know inch by inch, intimately, in all seasons. How much can one heart hold of the strange land? One cannot know, but it goes deep. This sphere I have made for myself is large to contain all repetitions and variations—no longer does it find expression easily. Days end as they begin, yet each one describes a wider arc. I am sinking into this land small bit by bit. But please listen to me. I am leaving. The New Year has come, and though the signals still change and the buildings have not moved, though I ride out on you as always, I am leaving. Yet you seem not to notice. My breath frosts the air, the gloved hands grip the handles,

the bicycle wheel
makes the same circles
it made yesterday

and I am leaving. Please hear me.

When I go, will I take the road with me? Can I still travel down it years at a time? Or will it tear out part of me when I travel it the last time? When I leave the house, will I still walk down the hall? Will others notice the face staring back from the window as I do now? Can you be remolded to fit those others, you who have held my life? Now I must dismantle you; everything will be taken apart. When, for the landlord, you are clean, I will look at you one last time. Though there will be no chairs to sit on, no bedding on which to rest, nothing on the walls, not even cobwebs, I can still walk the floors and look at you. I will say then,

the old tatami
have been scraped of everything
but memories

yet I will not say good-bye. I will never say good-bye.

Notes

Page 24—

The four major cities on the island of Shikoku are Takamatsu, Tokushima, Kochi, and Matsuyama. Each is three to three-and-a-half hours apart by train. Shikoku is about three hours by ferry from Ōsaka.

Page 28—

The loop line is a commuter train line that circles through Ōsaka. Umeda is a major stop on the line. Several other train and subway routes intersect there.

Page 30—

The Taira military clan, also known as the Heike, assumed control of Japan in 1159 by defeating the rival Minamoto clan, also known as the Genji. The Taira continued to reside in Kyotō and adopted the cultured ways of the capital's courtiers. After only twenty years, the resurgent Minamoto swept the Taira from the capital and, in the space of five years, utterly destroyed them. One of the great battles of that war occurred at Suma.

Page 57—

Jōshū is the name for present-day Gunma Prefecture, about 70 miles northwest of Tokyo. It is mountainous and one of the few regions in Japan not adjacent to the ocean. Kantō is the huge central plain surrounding Tokyo. Tokyo, Chiba, Kumagaya, Yokohama, and Kamakura are all in the Kantō area.

Page 61—

Enkakuji has perhaps the most spacious grounds of any temple in Kamakura. It contains numerous halls and a huge bronze bell and is still in active use.

Page 62—

Oni-oshi-dashi, literally "demons pushing-throwing," is an extensive area of piled-up obsidian slabs, each slab larger than a human being. The phenomenon was probably the result of volcanic activity.

Page 65—

Kannonyama is a large mountain outside Takasaki City. It is named after Kannon, the goddess of mercy. A huge concrete statue of the goddess stands at the top and can be seen from miles away. A large cherry grove nearby the statue is also well known locally.

Page 67—

For 148 years Kamakura was the Japanese seat of government, and many temples were built there. One famous temple features a hollow bronze buddha about twenty-five feet tall that can be entered through a small door at the base. Kamakura is a common site for fall school trips.

Page 68—

Go is a popular strategy game in the Orient. The board is a grid of nineteen lines by nineteen lines. Black and white stones are alternately placed on the intersections in an effort to seal off territory. Black always plays first.

Page 69—

Tatami are woven rectangular straw mats. They are used in place of carpets, and most floors in a typical Japanese house are covered with them.

Middlewood Press also publishes a quarterly haiku magazine edited by Richard Tice, Jack Lyon, and Lorraine Harr. It is called *Dragonfly: East/West Haiku Quarterly* and features contemporary English haiku, translations and explications of modern and classical Japanese haiku, contests, *sumie,* and calligraphy. For more information, contact Richard Tice or Jack Lyon at *Dragonfly,* 7372 Zana Lane, Magna, UT 84044. Also ask about the haiku poet chapbook series and the card game *100 Haiku Poets*.